A Field Guide to
"A Guide to Dungeness Spit"

A Field Guide to
"A Guide to Dungeness Spit"

by

Laurie Ricou

OOLICHAN BOOKS
LANTZVILLE, BRITISH COLUMBIA, CANADA
1997

Canadian Cataloguing in Publication Data

Ricou, Laurence, 1944-

A field guide to A guide to Dungeness Spit

Includes bibliographical references.

ISBN 0-88982-165-8

1. Wagoner, David. A guide to Dungeness Spit. 2. Dungeness Spit (Wash.)—Poetry. 3. Northwest, Pacific—Miscellanea. I. Title.

PS3545.A345G8437 1997   811'.54   C97-910899-3

THE CANADA COUNCIL | LE CONSEIL DES ARTS
FOR THE ARTS | DU CANADA
SINCE 1957 | DEPUIS 1957

The publisher would like to acknowledge the support of the Canada Council for the Arts for our publishing programme.

Grateful acknowledgement is also made to the BC Ministry of Tourism, Small Businesss and Culture for their financial support.

Published by
Oolichan Books
P.O. Box 10, Lantzville
British Columbia, Canada
V0R 2H0

Printed in Canada by
Morriss Printing Company Limited
Victoria, British Columbia

For

all those who have guided my own border-crossing, especially Glen and Rhoda Love, Bob Thacker, Fran Kaye, Kieran Kealy, Michael Peterman, Anne Rayner, Kim Stafford, Sherrill Race, Peter Taylor, Smaro Kamboureli, Bill New, Joel Martineau, Linda Ross, Bill and Nancy Latta, Cheryll Glotfelty, and Nancy Pagh; the many students who have taught me in versions of English 426, 438, 492 and 545 at the University of British Columbia; my colleagues and friends in the Western Literature Association; and the people who have walked with me on the Spit—the members of the Vancouver Magic, Ron Smith, Bob Kroetsch and Treva Ricou.

Acknowledgements

Guide books typically address the beginner and novice, the visitor rather than the experienced local. A field guide which is itself compiled by a visitor (to American poetry, to bird-watching, and to Dungeness Spit) will be unusually dependent on the expert help of others. Much of the collaboration which created this book will be evident in the list of works from which I have quoted, often without comment, and in the long walk of my dedication. For other crucial forms of collaboration, I thank Lynda Miller who did the keyboarding for many versions of the guide; to Angel Lam and Dale Yamaura, who cheerfully assisted with the correspondence; and to Alanna Fero, Carol McConnell, and Marian Gracias, three perceptive and tenacious research assistants, who risked sharing some of my emotional commitment to poems and places.

Several libraries provided me with congenial places in which to ponder: University of Washington Library, especially its Special Collections and Pacific Northwest Collection; the British Columbia Provincial Archives; the Oregon Historical Society; the University of British Columbia Library; the Sequim-Dungeness Museum; and Washington University in St. Louis, where I spent a marvellous week immersed in David Wagoner's papers. To the staffs of these institutions, my great thanks for your patience and advice.

Harriet U. Fish, dedicated local historian from Carlsborg, Washington, was a crucial guide in the Sequim-Dungeness museum: she ensured that a long table was spread with documents and clippings for our arrival, and remembered our visit by later sending me a dossier of photographs and a small twist of driftwood, the sand of the Spit still clinging to it. Maxine Miller of the Reference Department, in the North Olympic Library System, Marion Peterson of the National Archives— Pacific Northwest Region, and Jeff Logan, by e-mail from Port Angeles, added other essential documents or information.

Research funds from the University of British Columbia, and from the Social Sciences and Humanities Research Council of Canada, supported the work and allowed me to visit libraries, to present parts of the book as a performance for four voices (in Reno, Nevada), and to walk on Dungeness Spit.

No book would exist without the warm cooperation of David Wagoner himself. I hope this book will convey my enthusiasm for his poetry and for the Northwest places he has worded for us.

L. R.
27 October 1997

A Field Guide to "A Guide to Dungeness Spit"

David Wagoner

A Guide to Dungeness Spit

Out of wild roses down from the switching road between pools
We step to an arm of land washed from the sea.
On the windward shore
The combers come from the strait, from narrows and shoals
Far below sight. To leeward, floating on trees
In a blue cove, the cormorants
Stretch to a point above us, their wings held out like skysails.
Where shall we walk? First, put your prints to the sea,
Fill them, and pause there:
Seven miles to the lighthouse, curved yellow-and-grey miles
Tossed among kelp, abandoned with bleaching rooftrees,
Past reaches and currents;
And we must go afoot at a time when the tide is heeling.

Those whistling overhead are Canada geese;
Some on the waves are loons,
And more on the sand are pipers. There, Bonaparte's gulls
Settle a single perch. Those are sponges.
Those are the ends of bones.
If we cross to the inner shore, the grebes and goldeneyes
Rear themselves and plunge through the still surface,
Fishing below the dunes
And rising alarmed, higher than waves. Those are cockleshells.
And these are the dead. I said we would come to these.
Stoop to the stones.
Overturn one: the grey-and-white, inch-long crabs come pulsing
And clambering from their hollows, tiptoeing sideways.
They lift their pincers
To defend the dark. Let us step this way. Follow me closely
Past snowy plovers bustling among sand-fleas.
The air grows dense.
You must decide now whether we shall walk for miles and miles
And whether all birds are the young of other creatures
Or their own young ones,
Or simply their old selves because they die. One falls,
And the others touch him webfoot or with claws,
Treading him for the ocean.
This is called sanctuary. Those are feathers and scales.
We both go into mist, and it hooks behind us.
Those are foghorns.
Wait, and the bird on the high root is a snowy owl
Facing the sea. Its flashing yellow eyes
Turn past us and return;
And turning from the calm shore to the breakers, utterly still,
They lead us by the bay and through the shallows,

Buoy us into the wind.
Those are tears. Those are called houses, and those are
people.
Here is a stairway past the whites of our eyes.
All our distance
Has ended in the light. We climb to the light in spirals,
And look, between us we have come all the way,
And it never ends
In the ocean, the spit and image of our guided travels.
Those are called ships. We are called lovers.
There lie the mountains.

Dungeness Spit

*The longest natural sandspit in the United States thrusts 5
miles out from Olympic Peninsula bluffs into the Strait of
Juan de Fuca, so far that on a stormy day a walker feels wave-
tossed and seasick, and on a foggy day wonders if he's passed
over to another and totally watery planet. Birds run the sands
and swim the waters and fly the air. . . .*

*The trail ("no camping, no fires, dogs on leash, no guns, no
wheels") enters forest, then emerges to a viewpoint of spit
and Strait, joins the horse trail coming from the right, and
drops to the mouth of a nice little creek valley, in a scant 1/2
mile reaching the beach and the base of the spit.*

*So, there you are. Go. Via the outside route or the inside,
separated by the driftwood jumble along the spit spine. The
outside is the surf side, with views to the Panamanian mer-
chant marine sailing to and from the seven seas, to Vancou-
ver Island, San Juan Islands, Whidbey Island, and Baker-domi-
nated Cascades. The inside is the bay side, the first half a
lagoon, often glassy calm and often floating thousands of
waterfowl come to enjoy amenities of Dungeness National
Wildlife Refuge; the view is to mainland bluffs, delta of the
Dungeness River, and the Olympics. The best plan is to alter-
nate routes.*

Both end in the standard pretty government-issue light-

house, the foghorn, and the tip of the spit 1/3 mile beyond. A light has been on this site since 1857, earliest in the state.

Harvey Manning,
Footsore 3: Walks or Hikes Around Puget Sound 220-2

A Pile of Stones

As soon as he [Francisco de Eliza] had established a base of operations at Nootka, he dispatched Quimper in the Princesa Real *on a two months' exploration of the strait, which was found without difficulty. After spending more than a month examining Clayoquot Sound and other harbors along the northern shore, Quimper crossed to the south to investigate a tale told by the Indians of a wide channel leading off to the south and west. Coming to shore near a long sandspit (Dungeness Spit) he maneuvered to cross the bar into the harbor behind, but abandoned the attempt and anchored a half mile off shore. Here he remained for ten days, trading with the Indians who came alongside—exchanging "the King's copper" for sea otter skins; sending men ashore to fill the water casks and to wash clothes. First Mate Gonzalo de Haro was sent in the longboat, together with Second Mate Juan Carrasco in an Indian canoe (also purchased with the King's copper) to map the harbor behind the spit, which was given the name Puerto Quimper. The expedition leader himself went ashore near the sandspit to perform the act of possession:*

". . . laying hand on his sword which he carried in his belt, he cut with it trees, branches and grass, moved stones and walked over fields and the beach without contradiction from anyone, asking those present to be witnesses to it. . . . Then

immediately taking a large cross on their shoulders, the men of the vessel being arranged in martial order with their muskets and other arms, they carried this in procession, chanting a litany with all responding. The procession being concluded the commander planted the cross and erected a pile of stones at the foot of it as a memorial and sign of possession of all these seas and lands and their districts, continuous and contiguous. . . ."

So was the region claimed for Spain.

Ruby Hult, *The Untamed Olympics* 14

A Guide to Dungeness Spit

Although David Wagoner began teaching at the University
of Washington in 1954, the *Seattle Post-Intelligencer*
reported at the end of 1959 that none of his writing "[had]
been influenced by the Northwest." (Farrell) The publica-
tion of "A Guide to Dungeness Spit" in 1962 first signalled
Wagoner's imaginative control over a new and ancient
place. After six or seven years of "living an experience"
(Farrell), he felt ready to guide his readers through and
around the Northwest, his primary literary landscape ever
since. "A Guide to Dungeness Spit" is a crucial poem not
only because it marks Wagoner's emergence as the Pacific
Northwest's Robert Frost, but also because it is a fine guide
to Wagoner's approach to writing poetry. As Robert K.
Cording notes, the poem is "'essential' Wagoner. . . . a kind
of prototype for Wagoner's best poems, which are written as
a series of instructions for survival in life." (Cording 350)
How can we best read these instructions? First, read the
`field' of Dungeness Spit. Pause there, and listen to the
echoes of local knowledge. If we cross from field to guide,
stop, and overturn the poem. The best plan is to alternate
routes.

Final Exam

A guide to Dungeness Spit: a wildlife sanctuary extending seven miles into the Strait of Juan de Fuca on the Olympic Peninsula. First rough draft during final exam. at the time it felt like my final exam. a poem of crucial private importance.

[Typed notes for poetry reading.] *DWP,*
Ser. 6, Box 16, F. 256.

Why Do They Come Here?

Like people, migratory birds need food, water and shelter. Both Nisqually and Dungeness National Wildlife Refuges have abundant supplies of water and offer a smorgasbord of foods to suit a variety of avian tastes. Shorebirds may feast on mudflat invertebrates while goldfinches prefer the fluffy seeds of thistles and dandelions. These refuges also have protected places where birds can find shelter from high winds and storms, and where they are safe from harassment by people. Migratory birds use Nisqually and Dungeness at different times and in a variety of ways. Some birds come in the fall and stay through the winter, while others arrive in the spring to raise their young through the summer months. Other birds stop for only a few days to eat and rest before continuing their fall and spring migrations.

Fish and Wildlife Service, *National Wildlife Refuges of Puget Sound and Coastal Washington*

Guided Travels

Something in us resists a guide. Hence, the sometimes
hectoring tone, as the poet-guide has to persuade his
companion to see it his way. We would rather go it alone.
Unless, of course, real danger threatens. Do not proceed
beyond this point without a guide:

> The official warning, nailed to a hemlock,
> Doesn't say why. I stand with my back to it,
> Afraid I've come as far as I can
> By being stubborn, . . .
> . . . . . .
> Why should I have to take a guide along
> To watch me scaring myself to death?

David Wagoner, "Do Not Proceed Beyond this Point
Without a Guide," 170

Near Port Angeles

Jutting into the Strait of Juan de Fuca, some 15 miles east of Port Angeles and 6 miles from Sequim, the Dungeness Spit National Wildlife Refuge protects seals, waterfowl, shellfish, and the occasional human on its 7-mile stretch of beach. Unfortunately, the refuge is so isolated that it is virtually inaccessible to travelers without vehicles of their own.

Harvard Student Agencies, *Let's Go* 189-90

Those There

The typical guidebook formulation defines gross character-
istics—"Dungeness Spit is about 5½ miles long and juts
into the Strait of Juan de Fuca. It forms a salt-water lagoon
used as a rest stop by thousands of migratory waterfowl."
It delineates the controls on the visitor: "Refuge regula-
tions prohibit fires, pets, bicycles, guns and camping." (*Tour
Book* 120) It gives basic information, often in sentence
fragments, for the identification of species:

> *Hairy Shore Crab.* Hemigrapsus oregonensis. *To
> 1¹/5 in. (3 cm) across the back or carapace. Square,
> grayish-green carapace. Legs have conspicuous
> fringes of hair. Commonly found under rocks in
> protected intertidal waters.* (Harbo 29)

Viewed in this context, the 'guide' of Wagoner's title clearly
speaks more as a personal companion than a handbook.
Indeed, with his frequent imperatives, the speaker sometimes
seems a presumptuous director. The poem's dominant syntax,
the variations on the weak expletive construction, at first
reinforces this impression, as if some know-it-all can't resist
labelling (but not explaining) everything in sight.

But, while versions of the formula "those . . . are" appear
fifteen times in the poem, they convey as much hesitation

as conviction. The deictics ("those," "there"), which would be meaningful in conversation with someone leaning over and pointing, for the reader become substitutes filling out the sentence but not adding meaning. *What* are cockle-shells? The copula verbs convey existence, but no action. Instead of writing "Canada geese whistle overhead," a sentence which would convey the writer constructing his own literary landscape, Wagoner says "Those whistling overhead are Canada geese." The shift puts greater emphasis on trying to read the natural landscape, "there," in the external world. Wagoner wonders—has us wondering—about the terminology by which we name flora, and especially fauna.

The element of doubt becomes more evident later in the poem when the insistent formula shifts slightly in the line "This is called sanctuary." In context, a paradox hooks behind the term *sanctuary*. The Refuge may protect species, but it's no guard against the abrupt death of an individual bird. "Which is the sanctuary?" Wagoner wondered in his first draft. "The sea, the shore, or the cove?" (G 1) After this line, the passive form of *call* is repeated three times in the last nine lines , each time suggesting the teaching of language to a child, and an inherent questioning. "These are *called* houses"—but are not? *Why* are "those . . . called ships"? "We are called lovers"—but we realize the ironies.

Slight shifts in a repeated formula signal a thematic development: a hint of hesitation becomes a more open doubt. Similarly, only once in the poem does "those" become "these," emphasizing that the poem pivots on the line "And these are the dead." The dead, and death, are the most immediate, the most assertive presence in the poem—

everything else is "those," out "there." The broad sweep of
the line, suggesting many kinds of "dead," is very deliber-
ately crafted. In the second draft Wagoner had continued
the earlier formula: "Those are dead crabs." (G 2) In
reworking the line, he shows most definitely that the poem
is a guide to more than topography. It is a guide to loving
with an awareness of death, and to dealing with death in
love. The generalized "bird" which "falls" in the completed
poem is more definitely identified in the first draft: "Bones
and feathers, the red-beaked gallinule lately dead; but we
two were dead lately." (G 1) Despite the journey's
ending in the ascent to the light in the lighthouse, the
"guide['s]" responsibility is to "defend" "the dark," not
only to protect the dark from attack, but to uphold, to
support by argument and evidence, as in a court, the
presence of death, and the dead.

Sanctuary

*Although the oilport itself is to be located on Port Angeles'
Ediz Hook, its tank farm would be sited at Green Point, a
major feeder bluff for Dungeness Spit. The pipeline would be
trenched into the bottom of the Strait of Juan de Fuca for the
six-and-a-half miles eastward to Green Point, then drilled
into the cliff and up to the tank farm.*

*"We're very gun-shy about this," says Rex Van Wormer
of the Fish and Wildlife Service. "Green Point sloughs away
continually. It's a major contributor of sediment to Dungeness
Spit."*

*If the cliff must be bulkheaded or otherwise stablized to
protect the pipeline, Van Wormer feels it may be the critical
action that starts permanent erosion of the Spit. Already
narrow near the landward end due in part to the angle of
wave attack, the Spit is occasionally breached in winter storms.
With an adequate sediment source, Dungeness heals itself.
Without that source, Van Wormer says, increased wave ac-
tion through a breach would quickly eliminate the eelgrass
beds, shorebird habitat, and oyster farms of New Dungeness
Bay and Harbor. (Eelgrass is the staple food of black brant;
the Refuge was created to protect the brant habitat.)*

Nancy Thomas, "Goodbye Oysters, Hello Oil?" 27

Dunge Ness

low headland on S. coast of Kent, 10½ m. ESE. of Rye. ¼ m. from high-water mark is a lighthouse with flashing light (Dungeness) seen 17 m. 485 yards from the main lighthouse is a white flash-light seen 11 m. On the main tower is a fixed light (red and green) sectors seen 13 m. It has a lifeboat sta. and a Royal naval shore signal sta. (Bartholomew 227)

Speculations on the origins of the place name suggest that the spit contains a whole variety of landscapes. *Naess* in Old English means "a promontory, a headland, a cape" and derives from *nasu*, nose (English Place-Name Society 130). *The Concise Oxford Dictionary of English Place-Names* tells us that Dungeness was named from Dunge Marsh, which in turn comes from the Old English *Den*-ge `the valley district.' (Ekwall 146) Dene is sometimes thought to be a root because of its definition: according to the *The Oxford English Dictionary*, "a bare sandy tract by the sea." So Dungeness evokes mountain, and valley, and sand hill. Littered with the "ends of bones," it is also something of a pile of detritus. According to *The Place-Names of England and Wales*, "Dunge- is prob. Dan. *dynge*, `a heap, a pile (of dung)'. . . . Cf. Dinganess, Norway." (Johnston 239)

Goldeneyes

On the many arms and passages of Puget Sound in winter little groups of fairly large ducks with snowy under parts *and flanks, and* glossy black heads *are scattered over the water, diving and reappearing, or, when startled, flying swiftly over the water with a* sharp whistling of the wings. . . . *Golden-eyes feed largely on mussels and other shellfish, for which they dive, often coming to submerged flats close to shore. . . . In late winter and early spring the male Golden-eye elevates his head and neck with the bill pointing straight up, at the same time uttering a nasal note, which suggests the spee-ick of the Nighthawk. Then he jerks the head quickly back till it touches the rump, and then brings it forward, often kicking the water back at the same time and showing a flash of his orange feet.*

Ralph Hoffman, *Birds of the Pacific States* 49

Birds

Checklist available. The Fish and Wildlife service lists as the site's primary species "black brant, ducks, shorebirds." The checklist includes 28 "accidentals," among them yellow-billed loon, New Zealand shearwater, mute swan, gyrfalcon, skua, parakeet auklet, and skylark.

Not including these, 246 species have been recorded. Winter populations include up to 1500 black brant as well as arctic and red-throated loons, grebes, double-crested and Brandt's cormorants, Canada goose, mallard, pintail, green-winged teal, canvasback, greater scaup, common and Barrow's goldeneye, bufflehead, oldsquaw, harlequin duck; common, white-winged, and surf scoters; common and red-breasted mergansers. Also killdeer, surfbird, dunlin, black turnstone, sanderling. Many more species are seen in spring and fall migrations, while species such as rhinoceros auklet and tufted puffin are most often seen in summer.

John & Jane Perry, *The Sierra Club Guide to the Natural Areas of Oregon and Washington* 186-7

The Switching Road

As the hikers' gaze and path shift from windward to
leeward shore and back, "A Guide to Dungeness Spit"
alternates lines as short as four monosyllables —"stoop to
the stones"— with lines—"miles and miles"—stretching up
to fifteen syllables; from documentary statement to dis-
tracted meditation. On one side, waves and tides shift and
change; on the other shore floats the calm of "a blue cove."

But the "still surface" of the guidebook's deliberateness
is as likely to be abruptly, sometimes alarmingly, disturbed
as is the quiet of the lagoon. The potential for flash and
alarm is built into a syntax of short and long sentences, as it
is into the varied line lengths, and most intriguingly into
the surprising shifts of audience. The poem intermingles
guidebook and dramatic revelation. It opens with an
"objective" report in the historic present. The writer
personalizes the guide by narrating the sequence of the
hike, imagined as he and a companion experienced it, in the
first person plural, which includes the reader.

But with his only question, "Where shall we walk?" the
form shifts from narrative to dramatic monologue. For
most of the rest of the poem, a questioning, if unquoted,
interlocutor is implied, and the monologue finds drama in
an emerging, if already complicated, relationship between

lovers. Complicated in part because the poem invites the
realization that only one traveler gets to speak. Yet the
speaker shifts to the opening tenor ("we both go into mist")
often enough to keep us off guard. And as the shifts
surprise us, we begin to realize how neatly the poem blends
forms. It intones information and instructions with the
didactic deliberateness of William Carlos Williams' "Tract."
At this level, the speaker urges the reader to look at, and
listen to, the world up close, to discover the "inch-long
crabs," to imagine and share their story. But this teacherly
level is suffused in the dramatic monologue, the guide
evasively masking the "distance[s]" and "tears" of an
intensely intimate loving.

Lovers

*From the Dick family comes this anecdote of pioneer romance:
Three-year-old Mable [sic] Dick was supposed to be taking a
nap but instead hid in the wagon and went to Dungeness,
five miles away, with her father.*

*When she was missed, the older children were sent to search
for her in the woods. Sister Kate, crying and calling for the
little one, stumbled into the arms of a tall, husky stranger.*

*It was George Lotzgesell, who asked her why she was cry-
ing. They were married a few years later.*

Sequim Bicentennial History Book Committee,
Dungeness: The Lure of a River 172

The Grebes

Suddenly it leaps forward and disappears head first, rising later a short distance off. . . . A morning spent in watching a breeding colony in June or early July will disclose a fascinating variety of activities. Here a pair are diving and coming up with masses of green weed, with which they are building up their floating nest. Males are rushing at each other with lowered heads, or diving and reappearing near the female. Other pairs are engaged in striking courtship performances, swimming side by side, throwing back their heads and suddenly facing each other with their bodies erect, or in the same upright position rushing side by side along the water.

Ralph Hoffmann, *Birds of the Pacific States* 8

Dun

. . . I think the sea continually divides the world into dark and gleam, the northwest sky relieves us from the pressure of always choosing by being usually gray, but of course that's only theory. No real accounting for calm.

Richard Hugo, "Letter to Wagoner from Port Townsend" 293

Explanation

Dave Wagoner, who knows his way around in several art forms, poetry, plays, novels, painting, does not free his imagination from the logical prose-narrative relationships. He does not get off the subject, and he takes time for explanation— two habits of the prose writer that are lethal for the poet. None of this behind the backs of friends—have said this to them [Wagoner and Carolyn Kizer] already.

Richard Hugo to James Dickey, March 29 [1960?]

Ecological Pilgrims

Sequim—You stand on a bluff above the Dun-geness National Wildlife Rufuge, looking out at a thread of bland land that is one of the world's longest natural spits. Your eyes search the Spit and Dungeness Bay for some sign of life, or some sign of the disaster, for anything of significance.

You wonder why 172,000 people visited Dun-geness National Wildlife Rufuge last year. Visited what—from the bluff—appears to be a modest spine of sand and driftwood, only a few dozen yards wide in places, hooking 5½ miles out into the Strait of Juan de Fuca.

And why in the past few weeks—since Dec. 21, when the tanker ship ARCO Anchorage dumped more than 180,000 gallons of oil into nearby Port Angeles harbor—another 2,500 people have flocked to the natural mini-peninsula. They came like ecological pilgrims to a Northwest Mecca, wanting to see what had happened to their Spit.

On the bluff, you are, frankly, wondering why they care so much.

You don't yet realize that the Spit and Dun-geness Bay are biological powerhouses, resting and feeding and breeding grounds for hundreds of migratory species of birds. Or that the Spit is a participatory environment, that it is a complex and spectacular world which is invisible until you are close

*up, within it. Or that the effects of the oil spill are also al-
most impossible to see, but like life on the Spit itself, may
prove no less real for being invisible. In fact, although the
beaches now are clean, the spill may affect marine and bird
life here for months or years to come, or even affect bird
populations in other parts of the continent. . . .*

*"It's a biological smorgasbord," says [Ulrich] Wilson of
the refuge. "The bay is protected by the Spit from the weather.
That allows the water to be stratified, so that marine algae,
phytoplankton and fish larvae can thrive. It's a nursery for
immature salmon. Herring lay their eggs on eelgrass blades
. . . And it's all strategically located in the flyway of migrat-
ing birds."*

*"It's growing, you know," adds [Vern]Wray, "25 to 40 feet
a year."*

*You stare harder at the desolate landscape as Wray ex-
plains that driftwood is the backbone of the Spit, catching
sand and silt, which catches more driftwood, which makes
more Spit.*

*The Coast Guard lighthouse near the end of the Spit winks
back at you. When it was built, in 1857, it was at the very tip
of the Spit. Now, Wray says, there is another quarter mile or
so of sand and driftwood beyond it.*

*Most of the ARCO Anchorage's oil hit the Spit far out,
near the lighthouse, so that's where you must hike if you
want to see the effect. Heck, you think, 5 1/2 miles to the
lighthouse: a cakewalk.*

If spits could, you will think later, this one would, in your eye.

*After a half hour, it feels like you have been walking across
thickly iced cake. The sand mires your boots as you plod out
onto the Spit. The lighthouse floats like a distant mirage.*

To the west you see the plumes of the mills at Port Angeles, 15 miles away, scene of the ARCO Anchorage accident. The Spit now seems immense. The driftwood forms a tangled "Lord of the Rings" sort of wasteland. You are little on the endless lip of beach.

You can see the Spit tearing down and building itself up. The waves going out collide sometimes with the waves coming in, and there is an explosive clap. Then the water reaches up onto the beach and seizes the sand, along with skull-sized rocks, churning them loudly the way a giant might finger a handful of marbles.

The only signs of the oil spill are a good four miles out on the Spit. There is a VW Bug-size tree stump, the cut surface of which is beaded with water on oil. A little farther, there are oil streaks in the sand in half a dozen places: nothing substantial, just streaks. Out of sight.

But Wilson says the oil is there. The Spit, he says, eats up spilled oil, buries it.

"The feared effects of the oil spill," says Wilson, "are long-term chronic oil pollution. The effects are going to be very subtle, very long-term. I don't believe it will be the result of just the ARCO spill. We're talking 20, 30, 40 years from now. Unless we get our act together, and prevent what's happened here, it will be like the North Sea (where serious oil spills have occurred). Their seabird populations have declined. Shorebird populations have declined. There's been a decline in fisheries."...

"In 30 years," Wilson worries, "People are going to say, `What happened to all the black brant?' `I remember when we used to go clamming here.' It isn't going to be just the ARCO spill. You tell me there is not going to be another spill," demands Wilson.

39

But when asked, before he turns back to the mainland, what should be done, he sighs: "I don't know. I wish I did."

It's been 2 1/2 hours, and you get the feeling that you are being watched. Two harbor seals are spying on you from 20 yards off shore. They duck out of sight when spotted. By the time you finally are at the lighthouse there are 10 seals watching. They seem incredulous that you've walked all the way out here. You are incredulous, too.

Past the white tower of lighthouse is the caretaker's white house.

Inside, Coast Guardsman Don Williamson and his wife Vicki and 3-year-old daughter Krista are watching a color-TV set. They tell you tales of returning to the lighthouse on Christmas Day and seeing the 6-inch deep pools of oil.

"The birds were the worst," recalls Williamson. "All of them were trying to get to land, all covered with oil. I went down and picked one up with my bare hands, no net or nothing."

As a reward for making the Spit hike, you get to sign the lighthouse logbook, a yellowed tome with quilled signatures dating back to 1895. And you get a tour of the old lighthouse. You wonder aloud how many steps there are as you climb to see the new 1,000-watt bulb and take in the view. Without hesitation, Williamson replies: "74."

Williamson says that other than seeing birds and people, he has encountered only two other animals on the Spit. "I've seen a skunk," he says. "And one day a cat came to our door. I left some food out, but we never saw it again."

James Lalonde, "Dungeness Spit" E1, E4

Utterly Still

In reading newspapers, books, articles from and about the communities near the Spit—Whisky Flat, New Dungeness (now Dungeness), Sequim—you will be surprised to find very little reference to Dungeness Spit. Surprised because such a distinctive geological and ecological phenomenon seems to have been taken for granted, and seldom visited by the locals. The Spit is remote, inhospitable, uninhabitable. People here are a surprise.

People

Right here through irrigated farm lands to DUN-GENESS, 5.5 m. This picturesque fishing village spreads over a point jutting into Juan de Fuca Strait, a short distance east of a long sandy spit. Clumsy-looking power boats, their sterns piled high with traps, ply the coastal waters for crabs. These famed Dungeness crabs, exceptionally fine-flavored and firm in texture, are shipped in cold storage to Midwestern and Eastern cities. . . .

The inhabitants of Dungeness are a hardy folk, who have learned to respect the swirling eddies and strong tides of the Strait. In the days of wooden ships and sails many a ship piled up along these shores, and the settlers customarily kept beach fires burning brightly on stormy nights to warn navigators. They also formed a volunteer life-saving corps and pulled their stout boats through heavy seas to rescue the crews of shipwrecked vessels.

Work Projects Administration, *A Guide to the Evergreen State 548*

Graveyard Spit

No story associated with the Spit is told more often, and
consequently in more versions, than the story of the
Dungeness massacre. Although among the Clallam a
sandspit is the preferred site for a cemetery (Gunther 248),
it seems certain Wagoner has the story of the massacre in
mind when he announces to his companion, starkly and
enigmatically: "And these are the dead."

Treaty of Point no Point
Sklallam Agency
October 7, 1868

Hon. T.I. McKenny
Supt. of Indian Affairs
Olympia, W. T.

   Sir:
In accordance with your order of Sept. 28th I have the honor
to report the circumstances connected with the massacre of
(18) Chimsean Indians by a number of Sklallam parties to
this Treaty.
   On receipt of the above mentioned order I immediately
started for Port Townsend to obtain such information as would

enable me to detect the murderers, and on my arrival there I arrested one of the party, and from him obtained the names of the murderers and the following account of the affair—

It appears from their statements that a party of Chimsean Indians consisting of 10 men 8 women & 1 child left Port Ludlow for Victoria, the Port Discovery Indians hearing of this, concocted a plan to murder & rob them, and started for Dungeness to obtain the assistance of the Sequim Bay and Dungeness Indians (in which they were successful) in the meantime the Chimseans had camped on Dungeness Spit near the Light House and erected a sail tent to accomodate [sic] all 19, shortly after midnight the Sklallams cut the tent ropes and let the tent fall on the sleeping Chimseans, when one party of the Sklallams drew their knives and spears and stabbed them through the tent indiscriminately, the other party of Sklallams seized their guns and revolvers, and shot and killed all excepting one woman who secreted herself under a mat and thereby saved her life, during the massacre one of the leaders of the Dungeness Party named Tyee Sam went to one of the Chimseans (whom he Sam) supposed dead, for the purpose of robbing him, when the Chimsean jumped up seized a gun which was close by, and shot and instantly killed him, which with the exception of one or two cut heads was all the injury sustained by the Sklallam. One party of the Sklallams being located near Port Discovery and the others at Dungeness, I dispatched Mr. Jas G. Swan of Port Townsend to arrest the latter and bring them to this Reservation, while I started for Pt Discovery and arrested 9 of the murderers, Mr. Swan put out for Dungeness and yesterday brought 12 to the Reservation, making in all 20 prisoners which excepting 5 others who secreted themselves on our ap-

proach comprise all the murderers 20 of these I have this day confined in Block House awaiting further orders, the twentieth being so young I sent him in to the school with instructions to the teacher not to allow him to leave without my order...

These prisoners appear very much frightened and all say that they desire to bring their families to the Reservation.

They are also willing to make restitution of all property stolen from the Chimseans the night of the massacre, and are willing to have it paid from any annuity money which they are to receive.

In conclusion I would inform you that the Block House on this Reservation has not capacity for this number of prisoners and I would be glad if you could make some other disposition of them, I would also call your attention to the valuable assistance rendered me by Mr. J. G. Swan in making the arrest, and request your official recognition of his services.

> *Very truly sir*
> *your obdt Servt*
> *C.J. King*
> *U.S. Ind. Agt.*
> *Sklallam Agency*

In the aftermath of the massacre, the rivalry between the Tsimshian (from what is now Canada) and the Clallam provoked international tensions in the Dungeness area. *The Weekly Message,* published in Port Townsend, fumed "We sincerely hope that General McKenney will not pay another farthing to the Chimseans [in compensation for the massacre]. . . . We hope the Chimseans will come down and have a fight. The result would be their extermination and another item to be added to the already long account of Alabama and San Juan claims against the English government." (Lambert 4) In later years, however, another commentator would turn to a different authority in Victoria for this muddling clarification of the events which gave Graveyard Spit its name:

Provincial Arhives
Victoria, B.C.
May 3rd, 1962

Mrs. Irwin C. Harper
519 East 8th Street,
Port Angeles, Washington, U.S.A.

   Dear Mrs. Harper:

Your letter of April 17th regarding the Dungeness (Chimsean) Indian Massacre has come to hand, and we have been able to locate a number of contemporary newspaper references to this event in September, which I attach herewith for your information. There seems [sic] to be some differences in the information as you have outlined, and indeed between the various accounts which I should draw to your attention.

(1)Date. It appears to have occurred on either the night of September 20 or the early morning of September 21, 1868. September 20th was a Sunday and this would seem to fit newspaper references to Sunday or Monday.

(2)Number involved. This varies: 14, 15, 19; 15 (8 men, 5 women and 2 children). All accounts agree that one woman escaped death. Presumably the report of the Commissioner

of Indian Affairs fixing it at 17 as you cited would be correct. In spite of the reference in this report to the massacre have been [sic] *"reported to the Commissioner last year," there appears to be no printed version. The agency report for the previous year is dated August 1868, before the massacre had occurred and the Report of C.S. King dated August 15, 1869 (in Report of the Commissioner of Indian Affairs: Washington, 1870, pp. 140-141) makes no reference to the event. So presumably the figures in McKenney's account must have come from another report by King to the Commissioner. Possibly this would be in the files in Washington, D.C.*

(3)The Survivor: There are a number of suggestions as to how she escaped: covered herself "with beach sand;" "secreting herself beneath a mattress;" "afterward went to the lighthouse for refuge;" "taken to the house of a white man;" "swam to the mainland." According to the Port Townsend Weekly Message, *July 28, 1869, she was "subsequently sent to Fort Simpson by General McKenney" but there is no confirmation of this in the Victoria* Colonist, *nor in the histories of the Metlakahtla we have checked.*

(4)Motive: The newspaper accounts all agree that it was "for money;" the Washington Historical Quarterly *article you cite suggests no motive nor does the official Report of the Indian Commissioner. We can find no contemporary evidence to support the romantic tale by Mrs. Vincent.*

I trust this will be of some assistance to you.

> *Yours sincerely,*
>
> *Willard Ireland*
> *Provincial Librarian and Archivist*

Skysails

*In the forenoon as we went along Canoes came off
to us here & there from the Shore with Sea Otter
Skins for which they askd Copper or Cloth, but they
were able to keep with us a very short time as we
had a fair fresh breeze. . . .*

*We were not above 18 leagues from the Entrance,
when the Streights widend out to 9 or 10 leagues
across, we however continud our course along the
southern shore & in the evening went round the
point of a low sandy spit which jutted out from it in
very shallow water, when we came to an anchor on
the East side of it in 14 fathoms fine black sand
about half a mile from the spit which appeard a
long ridge of sand strewd over with a good deal of
drift wood & some high poles kept erect by four or
five supporting poles round the bottom of each—
What was meant by these we were at a loss to de-
termine.*

Archibald Menzies, *Journal of Vancouver's
Voyage* 16-17

*New Dungeness.
Pta. de Santa
Cruz, Caamano,
1790.*

*The poles for
nets used to trap
birds as
mentioned by
Scouler, 1825,
and many
subsequent
travellers.*

Spirals

The geese at the brim of darkness are beginning
To rise from the bay, a few at first in formless
Clusters low to the water, their black wings beating
And whistling like shorebirds to bear them up, and calling
To others, to others as they circle wider
Over the shelving cove, and now they gather
High toward the marsh in chevrons and echelons,
Merging and interweaving, their long necks turning
Seaward and upward, catching a wash of moonlight
And rising further and further, stretching away,
Lifting, beginning again, going on and on.

David Wagoner, "An Offering for Dungeness Bay" 201-02

Spit in the Ocean

*Each player gets four cards, dealt one at a time face down.
The dealer then places one card face up in the center of the
table. This card is wild, and every other card of the same
rank is wild. The card thus shown in the center of the table is
considered to be the fifth card of every player in the game.*

Richard Frey, *According to Hoyle* 19

"Boy collecting water. Playing spit in the ocean." writes
Wagoner in his prose notes for the poem. Spitting in the
ocean is defiant but desperate futility. Life is a game of
poker where all the players hold the same wild card. A spit
in the ocean is a gamble.

Mirage

The tall 100-foot tower became a popular day mark because the low spit was difficult to range on and many masters sighted it too late to come about. As built originally, the top half of the tower was painted with dark grey lead while the bottom was white in colour. The resulting optical effect caused some consternation to sailors. When viewed in daylight from a distance, the lighthouse had the habit of changing shape. At times appearing up to five times its normal height, it would change swiftly into a narrow black line on the horizon.

Donald Rutherford, "New Dungeness" 37

Bones

. . . the lighthouse was badly needed at the time it was built in
1857. There were many wrecks near the spit in those early
days; so many in fact, that it was known as 'shipwreck spit.'

Anonymous, "Dungeness Lighthouse" 23

Indians in strong tribes peopled the beaches, their village be-
ing on the sandspit later known as Clines Spit. Their dead
were buried in shallow graves on top of the ground similar to
the mounds of the Dakotas. A few were buried near the edge
of the high bluff near the McAlmond and Abernathy home-
steads and relics of these inhabitants are often turned up by
the plow, since that soil has been put to use for farming pur-
poses.

Mrs. George Lotzgesell, "Pioneer Days" 264

Every village has a cemetery, preferably out on a sandspit,
but it might be in the woods. On the sandspit a scaffold is
erected about two or three feet high and the body is laid on it,

sometimes covered by a small shed. The shed is just large enough to cover one body, for two corpses are never buried together unless it be a mother and infant who died at the same time. Posts two or three feet high are erected to hold a canoe containing a body. Again the body may be laid on the sand and covered by a canoe or a shed.

Erna Gunther, "Klallam Ethnography" 248

Out of wild roses, down from the switching road, out of

We step to this tongue of land built of tossed rooftrees.
[Didn't] I say we would? Floating on trees,
The water turkeys, wings cocked like skysail, move
  in the leeward cove,
And now we print lightly over the hump to the sea.
Seven curved miles to the lighthouse, all of it
  white and gull, the grebes
Dive in the leeward calm, On the windward
shore, the combers break. Day shine
The snowy plovers hustle past tidal pools. Are
  they young of other birds or their old selves?
Or simply the young of themselves, the white on white?
Crabs inching their own widths, tiptoeing sideways
  their pincers poised.
The whistling flights of geese going to sea. Which
  is the sanctuary? The sea, the shore, or the cove?
Bones and feathers, the red-breasted gallinule lately
  dead, but we too were dead lately.
The mountain disappears, and a boat of mist
  crosses the spit, whitens the high bluff.
Seven miles, and I end in light. We climb to
the light, spiralling to the top, and look, we have come
all the way, and the search is bright in our eyes.

The first draft of Wagoner's original manuscript

The Search

The first draft of "A Guide to Dungeness Spit" is written in pen on the back of the envelope in which a set of Wagoner's examination papers were apparently sealed. It is the only holograph draft in the Wagoner Papers at Washington University. The untitled draft has fourteen long lines, none of which contains the formula "Those . . . are," which became so crucial to the published version. As Wagoner revises, he works to develop the speaker's character and the drama of his monologue.

Despite its being one-third the length of the eventual poem, the first draft is a fine guide, beginning and end, to the process of Wagoner's writing. The draft opens very similarly to the published poem:

> Out of wild roses down from the switching road out of
>   pride
> We step to this tongue of land built of tossed
>   rooftrees. (G 1)

Commas after "roses," "road," and "pride" are scribbled out: although Wagoner is unusually lucid among contemporary poets, he likes the syntactical blur (the sense in which "roses" might be "down," for example) which can result from such variations. "Tossed" and "rooftrees" are used later in the poem.

Two changes of phrase are particularly interesting. Replacing "out of pride" with "between pools" keeps the poem focused on the symbolic possibilities of the literal experience of the landscape. Of course, the preposition "between" is repeated at the end of the poem—"pride" may be part of the "distance" between two lovers, but the poem is richer in possibilities for leaving such allegorical potential covert.

The holograph draft ends with a very long line:

> Seven miles, and it has ended in light. We climb to
> the light, spiralling to the top, and look, we have
> come all the way, and the search is bright in our
> eyes. (G 1)

Originally, that is, the poem ended urgently with an imperative, intimately, and in the popular sense 'poetically,' with a reified abstraction (search) ironically imaged in intangible light. In later drafts, the language of the "guide" becomes more prominent, and the relative remoteness of didactic labelling takes over the end of the poem, resulting in a flatter, almost bored and flaccid ending. The change diverts a potential sentimentality: Wagoner has turned to more of a non-ending, a stop without closure, to mirror in form a deepening awareness that the Spit is continuously growing and reforming: "it never ends/In the ocean."

Out of wild roses

Interwoven with its place in Paradise and with its symbolism of love and the mystery of life, is the rose's association with death. . . . The rose's association with death takes on a less spiritual side when one realises that the battlefields of history have become 'rose gardens.' Roses have, quite literally, sprung from the blood of slain heroes. For example, after the battle of Roncevalles in the 9th century, where Charlemagne's nephew Roland and his *douze pairs* of knights fell to the sword of the Infidel, wild Dog roses appeared, covering the mountain pass where the conflict had taken place. In fact the Spanish name for this wild rose is *fior dei escarmujo*, flower of the skirmish. Again, after the battle of Towton, where the Yorkists defeated the Lancastrians in the Wars of the Roses, a wild rose sprang up in the field which will not tolerate transportation from its blood-soaked bed.

Rosamund Richardson, *Roses: A Celebration 67-9*

Spits and Bars

a. The regulations set forth for marine beaches shall also apply, when applicable, to spits and bars.

b. The area inland from a spit or bar is protected from wave action, allowing such forms as shellfish to reproduce and live protected from the violence of the open coast. No activity which would jeopardize the ecology of this area is permitted.

c. The removal of sand, for commercial purposes, rock, driftwood, or an attempt to cut a passageway across a spit or bar will not be permitted.

Clallam County Shoreline Advisory Committee,
Clallam County Shoreline Master Program

Border Crossing

A lively traffic [from Dungeness] was carried on with Victoria. English sailors paddled silently across the wide Strait of Juan de Fuca after deserting their ships. Some took farms in this rich new land and became American pioneers. Chinese were smuggled over in boats. When the law, in the form of a government cutter, threatened, the Chinese were chucked overboard.

James Frits, *Seattle Times* 22 May 1949

Bodies

All the Chinese who attempted to reach the peninsula did not live to be potato farmers, and some were destined for disaster. Many were smuggled into the country in the late 1800s and early 1900s. Oldtimers told of a fast ship bringing a load of Chinese from Victoria into Dungeness Harbor. The government revenue cutter was too close and the captain dumped the Chinese overboard. Some of the bodies washed ashore on Graveyard Spit and the white people buried them. Later some of the bodies were claimed by relatives from China who took them home for burial. The late Richard Blake, son of the first keeper of the Dungeness Light, was one of the oldtimers who told the story.

George Hansen told the story of a man who disturbed the graves of Chinamen burried [sic] on the Spit. Bow Shee told him not to do it for if he dug up the graves he wouldn't live very long. The man went ahead, and two weeks later was killed when he drove off the Burlinghame Bridge.

Sequim Bicentennial History Book Committee,
Dungeness: The Lure of a River 154

Palette

The Clallam village at the mouth of the Dungeness River
was called Tsuq, meaning 'muddy' and referred to the
colour of the water. (Gunther 178) With the exception of
the "blue cove" earlier in the poem, Wagoner keeps to a
typically restrained Northwest colour scheme of sand and
mist—throughout the poem, he remembers the "yellow-
and-grey," "the grey-and-white." The colouration of birds
in view might be thought to be "bleaching," like the
rooftrees. The "bustling" snowy plovers (their name
derives from the Latin *plovarius*, belonging to rain, *OED*)
reconfigure the snowy owl which presides over the poem's
ultimate wisdom. Similarly the owl's "flashing yellow
eyes" (the snowy owl has a yellow iris, Hoffmann 169),
mirror the "goldeneyes" earlier in the poem, sustaining the
colour scheme announced at the outset. Thus, Wagoner
attentively plays the colours of the birds against what one
might call the colour narrative of the poem—across the
grey sand and through the grey mist, past the "whites of
our eyes" to the (presumably) yellow beacon of the light-
house, flashing its caution and guidance to all who are
navigating their lives.

Cormorants

When their goal is reached, they either splash into the water and sit with neck up and bill pointing at an upward angle, or light on a buoy, a boat or a rock among a row of their erect black companions. . . . When perched, Cormorants often sit with wings spread, occasionally shaking them.

Ralph Hoffman, *Birds of the Pacific States* 19

Snowy Plovers

On the outer beaches, between the lines of kelp left at high tide and the sand dunes, at any season of the year small whitish birds run so rapidly before an intruder that their short feet fairly twinkle on the sand.

Ralph Hoffmann, *Birds of the Pacific States* 101

With-In-Nature

This is a major poem by any standard and the first that we can imagine no other poet of our time having written. In it, the voice we hear not only is content with "the old words" but demands to be taken as literally as we would take the directions in a guidebook, or the words of a professional guide leading a guided tour.... We follow and are told what it is we are seeing, needing to be told because we are city-born and unfamiliar with the earth.... As we approach the end of the spit and look back at the land behind us, we find that the once-taken-for-granted has become strange, needing to be identified by our guide as the birds and the shells on the sand have been.... These objects too are a part of the nature we have been exploring.

Hyatt Waggoner, *American Visionary Poetry* 185

Fishing Below the Dunes

At Dungeness they troll for spring salmon as soon as the run comes inside the spit, using cockles for bait. The hook is made of two pieces of elk bone crossed at an acute angle and tied with elk sinew. The end of the shorter bone is sharpened to receive the bait. The line is of kelp about five fathoms long with a stone sinker in the middle and the hook at the end. Trolling is done from a canoe in the morning and evening.

Erna Gunther, "Klallam Ethnography" 200

Afoot

"Where shall we walk?" the speaker asks his companion in
the only interrogative in the poem. (There are *five* ques-
tions in G 1.) The only way to see the spit is on foot. The
poem's way of *knowing* Dungeness Spit depends on this
constraint: as a narrative of moving through space, and as
exploration in the language of walking. "It can be hiked to
the end, . . . by anyone in reasonable condition," notes one
travel writer. "But it is well to remember that the walking
includes much sand, which slows the pace." (Brown J4)

Wagoner slows the pace with long lines and frequent
caesurae: "First, put your prints to the sea,/ Fill them, and
pause there:" This odd formulation is one aspect of a subtle
pattern of pedestrian suggestions throughout the poem,
from the stepping in line 2, to the "tiptoeing" crabs to the
"climb[ing] . . . in spirals" at the end of the poem. Perhaps
most striking are the "others" who "touch" the fallen bird
"webfoot or with claws,/ Treading him for the ocean."

This line, changed from "They are fond of oceans" in the
last draft, is a good example of Wagoner's turning to
analogues of 'walk' to reinforce the notion of the full-day
hike which is necessary for any close human encounter with
Dungeness Spit. The image conjured up, of huge heavy(?)

birds crushing another bird, strikes a grotesque note. It
suggests a cruelty and oppressiveness in the life of nature
(the treading is *for*, perhaps 'on behalf of,' the ocean), which
intensifies the parodox of "sanctuary" in the next line. In
its declarative plodding, Wagoner's phrase "utterly still" fits
the tone of the poem well; yet, evidently, beneath the feet is
a dark brutality that disrupts all stillness.

The Bird on the High Root

As a child I was powerfully moved at my first meeting with a large owl. I was exploring a dimly lighted loft in a barn, when, peering into an empty cask, I met its eyes fixed on mine—a strange monster of a bird with fluffed, tawny plumage, barred and spotted with black, and a circular, pale-coloured face, and set in it a pair of great luminous yellow eyes! My nerves tingled and my hair stood up as if I had received an electric shock. Recalling this experience, the vividness of the image printed on my mind, and the sense of mystery so long afterwards associated with this bird, it does not seem strange that among all races in all parts of the globe it should have been regarded as something more than a bird, and supernatural
—a wise being, something evil and ghostly, a messenger from spirit-land, and prophet of death and disaster; the little sister or some other relation of the devil; and finally the devil himself.

W.H. Hudson, *The Book of a Naturalist* 154-5

Winter Brother

Directly opposite to our point of view the mountains back of Dungeness reared their heads covered with the sombre hue of the dark green forest of firs, and beyond them were the snowy peaks of the Coast Range, seeming to pierce the sky with their sharp, silvery crags. To my right was Protection Island, looking as bright and tranquil as if never storm had swept over its surface. Far in the distance down the straits, could be seen the light-house on the spit of Dungeness, a white speck no bigger than a man's hand, a pillar of cloud (or like a little cloud) by day, and a pillar of fire by night.

James G. Swan, *San Francisco Bulletin* 17 June 1857.

The Dunge Ness Monster

Brainstorming the possibilities of a poem on Dungeness
Spit, Wagoner, presumably evoking the analogue Loch Ness,
jotted "dun-geness. . . . the dungeness monster." (G n)
Although hints of something monstrous and threatening
whisper in the poem, the dungeness monster does not
appear. It may not have been seen since 29 July, 1892, when
The Dungeness Beacon reported this sighting:

> *Yesterday morning while the steamer Monticello was
> coming from Angeles to this city, and was almost
> directly opposite Dungeness, Captain Oliver says he
> saw the straits lashed into foam. Drawing near to
> the surprise of the captain and all on board, a huge
> sea serpent wrestling about in the waters as if fight-
> ing with an unseen enemy, was seen. Captain Oliver
> estimates it to be about fifty feet in length and not
> less than four feet in circumference of the body. Its
> head was projecting from the water about four. He
> says it was a terrible looking object. It has viciously
> sparkling eyes and a large head. Fins were seen,
> seemingly sufficiently large to assist the snake
> through the water. The body was dark brown and
> was uniform all along. From what he says it would*

be capable of crushing a yawl boat and its occupants.

As the steamer passed on its course, the snake was seen disporting itself in the water. At the time the Straits were calm, and there could have been no mistakes in recognizing the object.

(Anonymous, *The Dungeness Beacon* 29 July 1892)

Spittin' Image

Any poet who assumes so often the guise of the guide obviously will not tease syntax like Gertrude Stein, or phonemes like Louis Zukofsky. Always, there is the conviction—or distant hope—that language can teach you how to get from a to b. But, as is any poet worth reading, David Wagoner is a 'language poet,' manipulating, however subtly, both the semantic spirals, and the surprises in sound. The prose notes that Wagoner often writes toward a poem show the love of language and play most overtly: "dungeness." he writes, as if to discover the grey-brown colour scheme of the Spit, or to recognize, uneasily, that somewhere beneath this place is a relentless demand for repayment. At the end of the same note, he hears the music of the three syllables: "dun is a hill fortress or a fortified edifice. ness is a promontory. (from rose) gen is born. snowy plover makes three low notes." (G n)

Echoes of these can just be detected in the published poem (in the "mountains," for example, that rise up like a fortress at the end of the poem). But the most obvious word plays in the poem itself are "we must go afoot when the tide is heeling," and the sly punning at the end of the poem: "It never ends/In the ocean, the spit and image of our guided travels." In the first instance, Wagoner manages to play the Spit's necessary pedestrianism into a suggestion of the slow deliberateness of the discriminating guide and poet (a foot at a time and by the foot which measures poetic rhythm), while the tide which is chasing closely at the visitors' heels is also literally healing the spit, bringing to it the eroded particles of the nearby cliffs, which will fill in any breaks.

The pun on "spit" is a little more tricky, mainly because the antecedent for "it" is indeterminate. Either "ocean" is the "spit and image," or "it" is. "Light" is the most likely referent, but the connection is hardly inevitable, and we can't help noticing that "it" is the tail end of "spit," a geographical feature which is continually growing and is, therefore, never completed.

Or "it" may refer to the Spit. And the Spit, which continually presents a choice of two contrasting routes to the same end, which is littered with the bones of the many dead, whose end can never be reached, arcs through a likeness of life's travels—travels which are recognized, even by the guide, to be "guided" somehow, by some unnamed, unarticulated guide. One dimension of this journey is "image," the detail of geography, flora and fauna—carefully described by a guide—and the other is "spi[ri]t," whose significance and there-ness is only dimly intuited by both speaker and listener. Another guidebook explains the background to this wordplay:

> **The spittin' image of.** The germ of the idea behind this phrase has been traced back to 1400 by Partridge.... [T]he expression "he's the very spit of his

73

father". . . . *may mean "he's as like his father as if he had been spit out of his mouth" but could also be a corruption of "spirit and image." If the last is true, it would explain the use of "and image" in the expression since the middle of the last century.* Spittin' image *would then be derived from "he's the very spirit and image of his father," that is, the child is identical to his parent in both spirit and looks. It's possible that both sources combined to give us our phrase for "exactly alike," which is also written* spit and image, spitting image, spitten image, and spit n' image. *(Hendrickson 499)*

There Lie the Mountains

About five in the afternoon, a long, low, sandy point of land was observed projecting from the craggy shores into the sea, behind which was seen the appearance of a well-sheltered bay, and, a little to the S.E. of it, an opening in the land, promising a safe and extensive port. About this time a very high conspicuous craggy mountain, bearing by compass N. 50 E. presented itself, towering above the clouds; as low down as they allowed it to be visible, it was covered with snow; and south of it, was a long ridge of very rugged snowy mountains, much less elevated, which seemed to stretch to a considerable distance. . . .

The low sandy point of land, from its great resemblance to Dungeness in the British Channel, I called NEW DUNGENESS.

George Vancouver, *A Voyage of Discovery* 509-10

Those Are People

The long slow walk to the end of the spit transports the characters of the drama into another world—an animal world where an interdependency with the environment is felt but not understood—a world of romantic self-absorption. In this altered state, the guide has to begin again to re-learn an old language, to note almost whimsically: "these are people." The phrase also suggests the ancient and emerging power of The (first) People. Concentrated on the south side of the Strait, but with some communities on Vancouver Island, the world of the Clallam was the place of the "strong people." (Swanton 22)

Letter to Wagoner

*And around the bend a way, Dungeness Spit. I don't need
any guide but the one I've got, the one you threw the world
like a kiss of wind ending hot summer, though of course I am
seldom called lover these days and in bad moments when I
walk the beach I claim the crabs complain.*

Richard Hugo, "Letter to Wagoner from Port
Townsend" 292

Dungeness Spit, 1995

Take guides for good measure,
Laurie and Treva, and follow Wagoner
past the wild roses, hear his voice
step to the sea, a passage
between tide and lagoon
a walk upon the sea to the lighthouse,
erect in our admiring minds.
Bob shouts, eureka! it's only spitting distance
between this intimacy of sand,
logs beached on our path,
grebes and gulls, goldeneyes and brant
in exuberant flight,
and light's sanctuary.
Lovers and friends, come
walk these driftwood dunes,
seven miles of song in the heart.

A beached log for a compass,
we walk, seven miles of singing
in our uncertain bones.
Even the eye sags,
wearing this immensity.
The times of sand.
Ron, tangled in direction,
points gulls and grebes and orcas
out to the lighthouse promise.
Laurie and Treva, the measured
guides, tell us Wagoner's lines,
lead beyond roses to the joined
and divided ocean.
We limp skyward.
The spit goes nowhere
straight to the heart.

    Ron Smith and Robert Kroetsch

A Note on References

David Wagoner's early papers to 1962 (*DWP*) are held by
Washington University, St. Louis, Missouri. In Box 3,
Folder 71 are three drafts of "A Guide to Dungeness Spit":
in order of composition, a holograph draft on the reverse of
a 9 x 12 manila envelope (G 1); a two-page double-spaced
typescript on Hammermill Bond (G 2); a one-page single-
spaced typescript on Hammermill Bond (G 3). In the same
Folder is a paragraph of preliminary notes (G n) for the
poem, which may or may not precede G 1. Where it is
necessary to refer to other sections of the Papers, I use the
abbreviations Ser. (Series), Box, F (Folder).

   "A Guide to Dungeness Spit" first appeared in *The
Hudson Review* 15:4 (Winter 1962-63): 527-28

Works Cited

Bartholomew, John. *The Survey Gazetteer of the British Isles Including Summary of 1931 Census and Reference Atlas.* 9th ed., Edinburgh: Bartholomew & Son, 1950.

Brown, Tom. "A Hike in the Embrace of Both Land and Sea." *The Seattle Times/Seattle Post-Intelligencer,* 28 July 1985: J4-J5.

Clallam County Shoreline Advisory Committee. *Clallam County Shoreline Master Program.* [Report] August 1976.

"Dungeness Lighthouse—Light from the Past." *Marine Digest* 53.43 (14 June 1975): 23-24.

Cording, Robert K. "David Wagoner." *Dictionary of Literary Biography: American Poets Since WWII Part II.* Detroit: Gale Research, 1980: 348-355.

Ekwall, Eilert. *The Concise Oxford Dictionary of English Place-Names.* 2nd. ed., London: Oxford University Press, 1940.

Farrell, Barry. "Northwest Novelists Win Recognition as Four UW Professors Score Top Successes." *Seattle Post-Intelligencer,* 27 December 1959: Pictorial Review 3.

Fish and Wildlife Service, United States Department of the Interior. *National Wildlife Refuges of Puget Sound and Coastal Washington* [brochure]. Olympia WA: Fish & Wildlife Service, Nisqually National Wildlife Refuge, n.d.

Frey, Richard L. *According to Hoyle: Official Rules of More than 200 Popular Games of Skill and Chance.* New York: Fawcett Crest, 1970.

Frits, James. "50,000 Hyacinths on Dungeness Farm." *Seattle Times,* 22 May 1949, Magazine 10.

Gunther, Erna. "Klallam Ethnography." *University of Washington Publications in Anthropology* 1.5 (January 1927): 171-314.

Harbo, Rick M. *Guide to the Western Seashore: Introductory Marinelife Guide to the Pacific Coast.* Surrey, B.C.: Hancock House, 1988.

Harvard Student Agencies, Inc. *Let's Go: The Budget Guide to Pacific Northwest, Western Canada, and Alaska.* New York: St Martins Press, 1989.

Hendrickson, Robert. *The Facts on File Encyclopedia of Word and Phrase Origins.* New York: Facts on File, 1987.

Hoffman, Ralph. *Birds of the Pacific States.* Boston: Houghton Mifflin, 1955.

Hudson, W.H. *The Book of a Naturalist.* 1924. London: J.M. Dent & Sons, 1928.

Hugo, Richard. *Making Certain It Goes On: The Collected Poems of Richard Hugo.* New York: W.W. Norton, 1984.

Hugo, Richard. Letter to James Dickey. 29 March [1960?]. James Dickey Papers. Washington University Library, St. Louis, Missouri. Ser. 1 B 3 F. 56.

Hult, Ruby El. *The Untamed Olympics: The Story of a Peninsula.* Portland: Binfords & Mort, 1954.

Johnston, James B. *The Place-Names of England and Wales.* London: John Murray, 1915.

Lalonde, James E. "Dungeness Spit: The Invisible Story." *Seattle Times,* 22 January 1986: E1, E4.

Lambert, Mary Ann. *Dungeness Massacre and other Regional Tales.* n.p.: author, 1961.

Lotzgesell, Mrs. George. "Pioneer Days at Old Dungeness." *Washington Historical Quarterly* 24.4 (October 1933): 264-70.

Manning, Harvey. *Footsore 3: Walks or Hikes Around Puget Sound.* Seattle: The Mountaineers, 1981.

Menzies, Archibald. *Menzies' Journal of Vancouver's Voyage, April to October, 1792.* Ed. C.F. Newcombe. Archives of British Columbia, Memoir N. 5. Victoria, B.C.: printed by W.H. Cullin, 1923.

Perry, John and Jane G. Perry. *The Sierra Club Guide to the Natural Areas of Oregon and Washington.* San Francisco: Sierra Club Books, 1983.

Richardson, Rosamond. *Roses: A Celebration.* London: Judy Piatkus, 1984.

Roethke, Beatrice. Christmas card to Dave and Patt [Wagoner]. 20 December 1964. David Wagoner Papers. Washington University Library, St Louis, Missouri Ser. 1 F.5.

Rutherford, Donald. "New Dungeness: Lighthouse on a Spit." *Northwest Sea* 68.9 (September 1976):37.

Sequim Bicentennial History Book Committee. *Dungeness: The Lure of a River: A Bicentennial History of the East End of Clallam County.* Ed. Virginia Keeting. Port Angeles WA: Sequim Bicentennial Committee/The Daily News, 1976.

Swan, James G. "Scenes in Washington Territory. Number Five. A Trip to Protection Island and Port Discovery." *San Francisco Bulletin,* 17 June 1857.

Swanton, John Reed. *Indian Tribes of Washington, Oregon and Idaho.* Bureau of Ethnology Smithsonian Institution Bulletin 145. 1952. Fairfield, Wash.: Galleon Press, 1979.

Thomas, Nancy. "Goodbye Oysters, Hello Oil?" *Pacific Search: Northwest Nature and Life* 12.8 (June 1978): 27.

"Too Close for Comfort: The Gray and Festive Sea Serpent in the Vicinity of Dungeness." *The Dungeness Beacon* 19 July 1892, 3.

Tour Book: Oregon Washington. Fall Church, VA: American Automobile Association, 1989.

Vancouver, George. *A Voyage of Discovery to the North Pacific Ocean and Round the World 1791-1795.* Ed. W. Kaye Lamb. London: Hakluyt Society, 1984.

Wagoner, David. *Collected Poems 1956-1976.* Bloomington: Indiana UP, 1978.

Waggoner, Hyatt H. *American Visionary Poetry.* Baton Rouge: Louisiana State University Press, 1982.

Work Projects Administration, Washington Writers' Program. *A Guide to the Evergreen State.* Portland: Binfords & Mort, 1941.

Postscript

P.S. I love that 'Dungeness Spit' poem.

Beatrice Roethke, December 20, 1964.

Permissions

About the Author

Laurie Ricou was born in Brandon, Manitoba, in 1944. He completed his BA at the University of Manitoba and his PhD at the University of Toronto. He is well known as a critic of Canadian literature, in particular for his unique approaches to the subject, as in his study of child languages in his book *Everyday Magic* (1987). For fifteen years, he was the Associate editor of the influential journal *Canadian Literature*, and in 1995 he was the first Canadian president of the Western Literature Association. His current project, tentatively entitled The Arbutus/Madrona Files, an extended work on the Pacific Northwest, once again explores his interest in border crossings, the complimentary and different responses of unique cultures to a shared region. Ricou is also an avid soccer fan and for the past eighteen years has coached women's soccer in the Lower Mainland of B.C. He is a teacher at the University of British Columbia and lives with his family in Vancouver.